I0454934

United States
Department of
Agriculture

Forest Service

Pacific Southwest
Research Station

General Technical
Report
PSW-GTR-232

October 2010

USDA

Using Forest Inventory and Analysis Data and the Forest Vegetation Simulator to Predict and Monitor Fisher (*Martes pennanti*) Resting Habitat Suitability

William J. Zielinski, Andrew N. Gray, Jeffrey R. Dunk,
Joseph W. Sherlock, and Gary E. Dixon

Authors

William J. Zielinski is a research ecologist, U.S. Department of Agriculture, Forest Service, Pacific Southwest Research Station, 1700 Bayview Dr., Arcata, CA 95521; **Andrew N. Gray** is a research forester, U.S. Department of Agriculture, Forest Service, Pacific Northwest Research Station, Corvallis, OR 97331; **Jeffrey R. Dunk** is lecturer, Department of Environmental Science and Management, Humboldt State University, Arcata, CA 95521; **Joseph W. Sherlock** is a silviculturist, U.S. Department of Agriculture, Forest Service, Pacific Southwest Region, Vallejo, CA 94592; **Gary E. Dixon** is a forester (retired), U.S. Department of Agriculture, Forest Service, Forest Management Service Center, Fort Collins, CO 80526.

Cover photo by Michael Schwarz, Rocky Mountain Research Station.

Abstract

Zielinski, William J., Gray, Andrew N.; Dunk, Jeffrey R.; Sherlock, Joseph W.; Dixon, Gary E. 2010. Using forest inventory and analysis data and the forest vegetation simulator to predict and monitor fisher (*Martes pennanti*) resting habitat suitability. Gen. Tech. Rep. PSW-GTR-232. Albany, CA: U.S. Department of Agriculture, Forest Service, Pacific Southwest Research Station. 31 p.

New knowledge from wildlife-habitat relationship models is often difficult to implement in a management context. This can occur because researchers do not always consider whether managers have access to information about environmental covariates that permit the models to be applied. Moreover, ecosystem management requires knowledge about the condition of habitats over large geographic regions, whereas most research projects have limited spatial inference. For example, research has revealed much about the habitat of fishers (*Martes pennanti*) at various research sites in California, yet this work has not been translated into practical tools that managers can use to monitor fisher habitat regionally, or to evaluate and mitigate the effects of proposed forest management on fisher habitat. This led us to create new habitat models that are intimately linked to agency approaches to forest monitoring and software tools used by forest managers to plan timber harvests and vegetation management. We created habitat models that were integrated with these approaches and tools that forest managers use for two purposes: to inventory forest resources (i.e., Forest Inventory and Analysis [FIA] plots) and to simulate the response of stands to harvest, fire, insects, disease, and other disturbances (i.e., Forest Vegetation Simulator [FVS]). In this paper we provide an example of how to assess and monitor wildlife habitat using FIA vegetation monitoring protocols. We also provide an example of how to integrate an existing FIA-based model of fisher resting habitat into FVS, software that simulates the effect of alternative silvicultural treatments on vegetation data collected from field plots. Using these tools we produce quantitative predictions of the status of resting habitat quality for fishers, and describe how it can be monitored over time. We also provide an example of the effect of vegetation treatments on predicted fisher resting habitat, which illustrates a process that can be used to understand, reduce, or mitigate the effects of these activities on fisher habitat. This work on the fisher provides one example of how habitat assessments for wildlife could be advanced if they were developed with management applicability and implementation success as a goal.

Keywords: Fisher, *Martes pennanti*, inventory, habitat, modeling, simulation.

Introduction

The conservation of imperiled species requires monitoring of their populations and the abundance and distribution of their habitats (Nichols and Williams 2006, Yoccoz et al. 2001). Monitoring changes in habitat suitability is particularly challenging for species that are inconspicuous and occur over large regions (e.g., Huff et al. 2006). Frequently, land managers need to adapt the results of small-scale autecological research studies on a target species for use in rendering decisions about the effects of some management activity on a species' habitat. This is a cumbersome process and one fraught with interpretation issues. Research projects that are relevant to habitat management decisions typically produce some form of predictive habitat model. These models are built by relating animal location to vegetation and topographic covariates to estimate the distribution and value of habitat within a study area. Researchers, however, often conduct their investigations in relatively small areas over short timeframes, and managers are tempted to extrapolate the findings outside the bounds of reasonable inference. Moreover, smaller scale study areas are often chosen because they contain high densities of the organism of interest but may not be representative of the variety of conditions to which the species is exposed. These problems can lead to errors in application. Perhaps more important, the researchers rarely use methods that are easily implemented within the forest planning platforms used by managers and decisionmakers. This is because the researcher's choice of predictor variables (the environmental covariates) is usually based more on what they think will affect habitat choice by the target species than by what variables are available to forest managers for use in applying the model. The researcher often creates a study-specific habitat sampling protocol (e.g., Zielinski et al. 2004) that does not lend itself to application or adoption by those responsible for forest management and species conservation. Moreover, the research investigation is based on assessing the status of environmental features within a single period. When the environment changes, owing to natural or human disturbances, there is no opportunity to update a model's predictions because it requires collecting new field data in the treated area.

Some research approaches, however, are less vulnerable to these shortcomings. It is possible, for example, to monitor categorical classes of wildlife habitat, and to evaluate the effects of silvicultural treatment on these habitats, when habitat is grossly defined as a set of particular vegetation or land-cover types (e.g., oak woodlands versus mixed-conifer forests) and is measured remotely via aerial photography or satellite imagery (e.g., Larson et al. 2004, McDermid et al. 2009, Vallecillo et al. 2009). These habitat relations, however, are crude, and such measures are sensitive only to major changes in vegetation type over time and are insensitive to the more subtle changes in vegetation structure and composition caused by thinning, small group selections, partial harvests, uneven management in general, and prescribed fire. In addition, the categorical habitat approach is often not repeatable and only focuses on landscape-level predictors, excluding important information that occurs at other scales of habitat suitability. An improved approach is to spatially model vegetation structure using forest inventory data and to classify wildlife habitat conditions in a geographic information system (GIS) (e.g., McDermid et al. 2009, Spies et al. 2007).

More difficult to assess are changes to the important, but localized, habitat elements such as nest sites or resting or roosting sites (Huff et al. 2006). These microhabitat features can be essential, but are exceedingly difficult (and expensive) to assess and monitor over large regions. Traditional research products, including several that the senior author (WZ) has co-authored (e.g., Slauson et al. 2007, Zielinski et al. 2004), also fail to provide managers with easily used quantitative tools to predict how alternative land management practices will affect the habitat values that are influenced by these microhabitat features. However, new initiatives are beginning to exploit the availability of government agency vegetation databases as the basis for predictive models (e.g., Dunk and Hawley 2009, Dunk et al. 2004, Fearer et al. 2007, Huff et al. 2006, Welsh et al. 2006).

We provide in this report an example of how wildlife researchers can produce results that can be fully integrated with (1) management agency programs that monitor vegetation status and (2) the existing software that simulates the effects of management alternatives on forest structure and composition. Using the fisher (*Martes pennanti*) in the southern Sierra Nevada as our example, we demonstrate a research program that is co-developed with the Forest Inventory and Analysis (FIA) forest inventory program (Bechtold and Patterson 2004) and the Forest Vegetation Simulator (FVS) (Dixon 2002, Wycoff et al. 1982) such that foresters, biologists, and planners can use routinely collected FIA data and FVS to assess the status of predicted fisher resting habitat **and** to evaluate the effects of alternative forest management scenarios on future resting habitat value. We provide examples of two applications: (1) monitoring the status and change of fisher resting habitat on public and private lands in the southern Sierra Nevada and (2) simulating the effects of alternative silvicultural treatments on fisher resting habitat in the Sierra National Forest in California. Our work complements the important related work conducted by Huff et al. (2006) where FIA/Continuous Vegetation Survey (CVS) inventory plots were used to estimate nesting habitat for marbled murrelets (*Brachyramphus marmoratus*) in the Pacific States. Their work provides the best example, to date, of developing a habitat model using institutional plot-based vegetation data to estimate microhabitat features over large regions.

Our approach, and that of other researchers beginning to appreciate this method, differs philosophically from the typical approach, whereby a researcher convinces the forest management and planning officials to adapt the reseacher's models and to measure the predictor variables originally identified by them. Instead, we yield to the greater potential of developing the research, from the ground up, using sources of vegetation data that are regularly collected for inventory purposes and that can be integrated into software programs regularly used by foresters and silviculturists to predict forest change.

Methods

Developing the FIA-Based Fisher Resting Habitat Model

The foundation for this work is a predictive resting habitat model for fishers in the southern Sierra Nevada that uses variables from the FIA plot sampling protocol as predictors. This work has been described previously (Zielinski et al. 2006) but will be briefly reiterated here and placed in context of the conceptual approach (fig. 1). We developed a predictive resting habitat model by comparing vegetation and topographic data at 75 randomly selected resting structures with 232 forest inventory plots from the FIA system in the southern Sierra Nevada. Fisher resting structures are important habitat features that are typically cavities in large-diameter trees and snags where a fisher seeks refuge during periodic resting bouts (e.g., Zielinski et al. 2004). Resting structures were located during the course of two studies on the resting habitat ecology of fishers in the Sierra Nevada. The first was conducted from 1994 to 1996 in the Sequoia National Forest in Tulare County (Zielinski et al. 2004) and the second from 1999 to 2000 in the Sierra National Forest, Fresno County, California (Mazzoni 2002). Animals were captured, fitted with radio-transmitter collars and tracked to their resting locations.

Vegetation attributes at fisher resting locations were measured using the FIA vegetation sampling protocol (Christensen et al. 2008, USDA Forest Service 2007) by centering the FIA plot on the resting structure. The FIA protocol involves the collection of vegetation data at four or five (see details regarding this variation on p. 5) subplots within a 1.0-ha circular footprint. Within each subplot, a nationally standardized set of attributes are measured or estimated, including live and dead trees, site productivity and topography, stand structure, and disturbance history. In addition, regionally important measurements are taken, including understory vegetation composition, the quantity of downed wood and litter, ground cover, and other physical features (see Christensen et al. 2008, USDA Forest Service 2007,

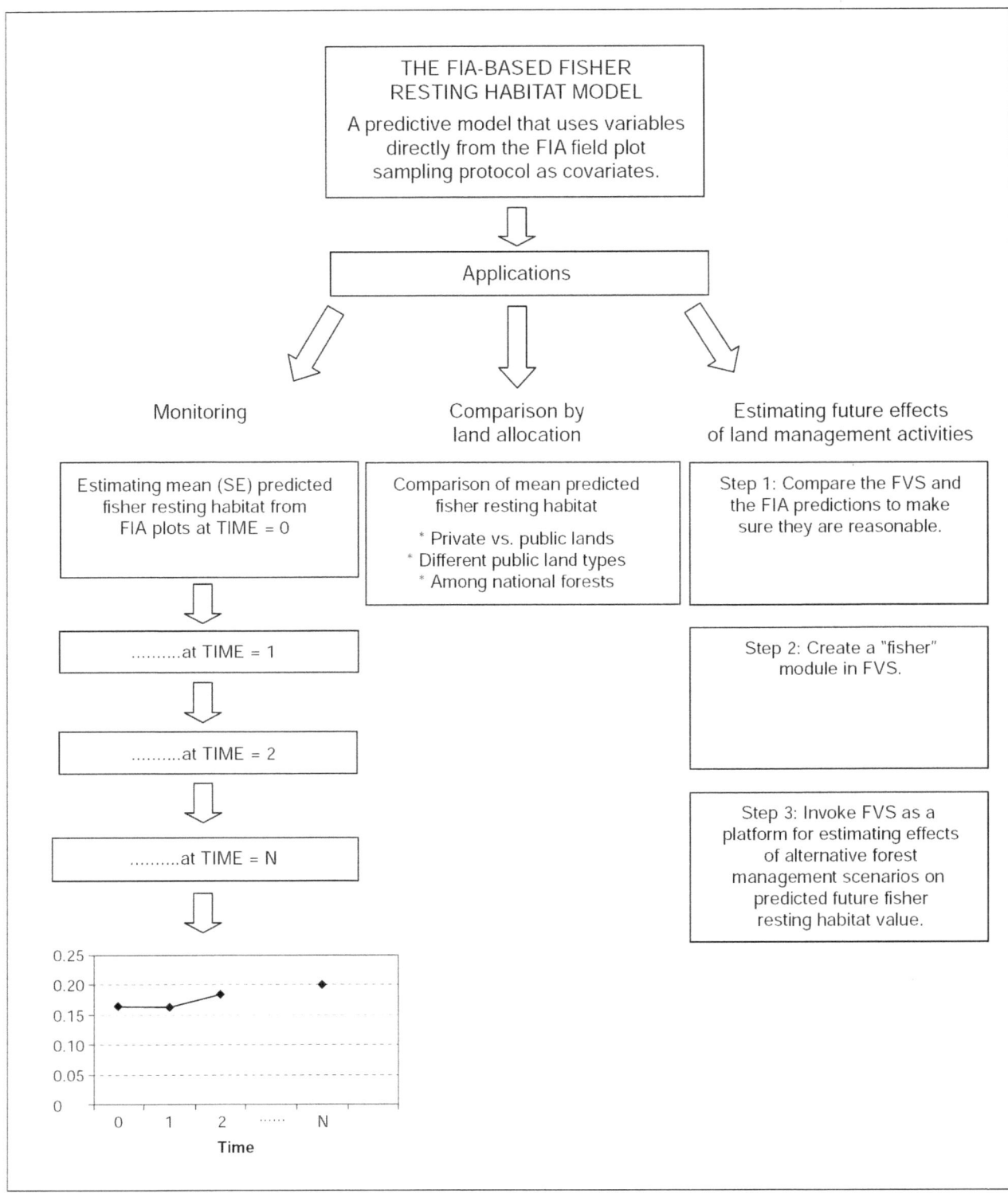

Figure 1—Conceptual diagram representing potential applications of a fisher resting habitat model linked to the Forest Inventory and Analysis (FIA) and Forest Vegetation Simulator (FVS).

http://fia.fs.fed.us and http://www.fs.fed.us/pnw/fia/publications/fieldmanuals.shtml
for details on national and regional FIA sampling protocols and data availability).

A predictive resting habitat model was developed by comparing characteristics
at the 75 plots centered on the resting structures with the characteristics of the
regularly sampled FIA points in the area. We limited the latter to include only
those plots within the approximately 2230-km^2 area within the range of suitable
elevations (1100 and 2300 m) (Zielinski et al. 1997) that also were within either
the Sierra Nevada or Sierra Nevada Foothills ecosection of the Ecological Unit of
California system (Bailey 1994). To model the distinction between resting plots and
available FIA inventory plots, we used nonparametric[1] logistic regression, specifically, generalized additive regression models (GAMs) (Hastie and Tibshirani 1990),
to evaluate a number of biologically feasible univariate and multivariate models
(Burnham and Anderson 2002). The best model captured most of the variation and
included the following variables derived from FIA plot information: overstory tree
canopy cover (CC), basal area of trees < 51 cm diameter breast height (dbh) (BA_S),
average hardwood dbh (DBH_HWD), maximum tree dbh (DBH_MAX), percentage slope (SLOPE), and the dbh of the largest conifer snag (CONSNG) (Zielinski
et al. 2006). Based on the functional forms of the partial response curves of each
predictor, we also estimated a parametric form of the best model (Zielinski et al.
2006). The nonparametric version (GAM) was used in the monitoring application
and the parametric version was used in all FVS applications.

Preliminary analyses: addressing changes in the FIA protocol—
The original FIA-based fisher resting habitat model (Zielinski et al. 2006) was
developed using a regional FIA field protocol that was revised shortly thereafter
with the adoption of new national standards. The original protocol was used in
the 1990s and included five subplots and variable-radius sampling of trees. The
FIA Program referred to it then as the "Region 5 [California] periodic inventory."
The revised (current) protocol is referred to as the "FIA annual inventory" and
includes four subplots and nested fixed-radius subplot sampling. The new protocol
is nationally consistent and viewed as a more efficient means for monitoring tree
growth and mortality over time. Because the stand-level variables in the fisher
model are aggregated at the plot level (i.e., subplot values are combined for each
estimate), they should not be highly sensitive to plot design. Nonetheless, a primary
concern regarding implementing the model, and using it for future monitoring of
fisher habitat, was whether the variables in the model were estimated similarly

---

[1] Parametric models assume that the variables can be characterized by some type of a
probability distribution, whereas nonparametric models do not rely on assumptions that
the data are drawn from a given probability distribution.

using the old and new protocol. To explore the extent of this variation, and to reassure us that the change in protocol would not be a problem, we selected 69 fully forested FIA plots on the Sequoia and Sierra National Forests between 1100 and 2300 m elevation that had been sampled using both protocols and had experienced no substantial disturbance (e.g., fire, timber harvest, avalanche). The majority of these plots were remeasured within 4 or 5 years so that the primary difference in the values for the vegetation variables, and in predicted fisher resting habitat value, was the difference in the sampling protocols. We used correlation analysis to evaluate the differences in estimated values of predictor variables and in the habitat values predicted by the model for the two sampling schemes. We expected some differences among measurements at each plot owing simply to the spatial variation in tree density and the different locations of the subplots; means and distributions of predictor values were used to indicate whether the change in plot design would affect the fisher model predictions.

Preliminary analyses: estimating the predicted resting habitat values in FVS—
The Forest Vegetation Simulator is a forest growth and yield forecasting system (Dixon 2002). It is an individual-tree forest growth model that has become the standard forest growth model used by forest industry and various state and federal government agencies, including the USDA Forest Service, USDI Bureau of Land Management, and USDI Bureau of Indian Affairs. Forestry professionals use FVS to develop silvicultural prescriptions, evaluate management scenarios, update inventory information, and provide input into forest planning models. Additional capabilities include forecasting vegetation structure, analyzing fire hazard, determining forest health risk, monitoring ecological processes, and carbon accounting (Dixon 2002).

It was necessary to reproduce, in FVS, the predicted fisher resting habitat values that were generated from the FIA plot data. Although the original fisher model was a nonparametric GAM, we also reported a parametric version of the best predictive model (Zielinski et al. 2006). We reasoned that providing a parametric version would make the model easier to apply, as it was a simple algebric expression, compared to the necessity of applying statistical software and loess smoothing functions, which are necessary using the GAM model to generate predictions with new plot data. The parametric version was created by evaluating the shapes of the response curves of each of the variables and substituting an approximate parametric form (e.g., linear, polynomial, logarithmic). Slopes and intercepts for the parametric function were estimated using general linear models. This version proved far easier to implement in FVS than the original nonparametric version and was used for all FVS applications.

Implementation of the parametric version of the fisher model in FVS was, however, not straightforward because of the challenge of replicating in FVS the values for some of the variables in the model. This process was simple for four of the variables, which were easily obtainable in FVS: basal area of trees < 51 cm dbh, average hardwood dbh, maximum tree dbh, and percentage slope. However, special effort was required to generate in FVS the values for percentage canopy cover and dbh of the largest conifer snag.

Calculation of tree canopy cover for the fisher model and in FVS used the crown width equations of Warbington and Levitan (1992), which use tree species and dbh as inputs. To be clear, we use canopy **cover**, the proportion of the forest floor covered by the vertical projection of tree crowns, and not canopy **closure**, the proportion of the sky hemisphere obscured by vegetation when viewed from a single point (Jennings et al. 1999). The original fisher model only included trees of predominant, dominant, and codominant crown positions and at least 30 percent crown ratio in the estimate of dominant tree canopy cover. In FVS, however, crown position is not an input variable, so the problem is estimating which trees should be included in the estimate of canopy cover. After trying various classification rules, we decided to use 50 percent of the height of the 90th-percentile tree in the height distribution on the plot as the lower cutoff point (which we referred to as the "50–90 rule"). By using the height of the 90th-percentile tree, we avoided biases caused by the predominant trees on some plots. We could not simply modify FVS to allow crown position as an input variable because, although this crown position would be true at the time the plot was originally sampled, we would not have an algorithm to model its change over time as we simulated **future** disturbances such as fire and silvicultural activities. Therefore, providing for crown position upon input is not enough; rules and methods to dynamically change a tree's crown position over time as other stand dynamics are happening would also be required. As an alternative, we used the "50–90 rule" to estimate which trees fall into the class from which canopy cover is estimated. Trees that met this standard, and which also were > 1 inch (2.54 cm) dbh and > 30 percent crown ratio, were included in the calculation.

We used the Fire and Fuels Extension (FFE) (Reinhardt et al. 2007) to track snags in FVS, including the dbh of the largest conifer snag, a variable in the model. The FFE does not track each snag separately, but tracks them in 2-in (5.08-cm) dbh classes. There are eighteen 2-in classes that track snags up to 36 in (91.4 cm) dbh; snags larger than 36 in become members of the 19th class. However, the FFE tracks heights of snags entering each class, and if the height difference is greater than 20 ft (6.1 m), then the class gets split into two classes. The dbh of the

7

largest conifer snag was estimated using the average dbh of the largest dbh class on plots that included a conifer snag.

To explore the magnitude of difference that occurs in the variables and the model output when using either the original FIA process for estimation or the process as replicated in FVS, we selected data from five FIA plots in the southern Sierra Nevada. We used these data to compare the original FIA estimated value with the FVS estimated value for each of the six predictors in the fisher model. We also compared the model output (predicted fisher resting habitat value) that was produced when (1) the original FIA method for estimating the variables was used versus (2) the FVS version of the variables was used. We sought to confirm, in particular, that our approximations for canopy cover and largest conifer snag would result in no substantial difference in the predicted resting habitat value when represented in FVS, compared with the original predicted resting habitat values in FIA.

Monitoring Status and Change of Predicted Resting Habitat

We used the GAM version of the best predictive model (Zielinski et al. 2006) to estimate relative resting habitat suitability at each of the FIA plots that fell within the 1100 and 2300 m elevation range within and near the four national forests in the southern Sierra Nevada: Eldorado, Stanislaus, Sierra, and Sequoia. Values of each of the six predictor variables in the best model were derived from the data at each plot and put into the GAM model to generate a predicted probability of resting habitat value that ranged from 0 to 1. We illustrate the monitoring value of these data by comparing the mean predicted values from plots that were sampled in the mid-1990s (the Region 5 periodic inventory) with those sampled in the mid-2000s (the FIA annual inventory). For the purposes of this example, we refer to the first period as "1997," the midpoint of the period 1995–1999 when the plot data were collected. The FIA annual inventory, which started in 2001 in California, is designed to sample 10 percent of the total plots each year, such that a monitoring cycle is concluded in 10 years. Thus, we refer to the midpoint of the second period (2001–2007) as "2004." Because the Region 5 periodic inventory implemented on national forests in California in the 1990s intensified the density of plots in strata defined from vegetation maps, and the annual inventory is based on a national fixed-probability grid of one plot per 6,000 acres (2430 ha), the number of FIA plots that were sampled in 1997 was substantially greater (n = 626) than in 2004 (n = 283).

Simulating the Effects of Silvicultural Alternatives Using FVS

An important feature of FVS is the event monitor, which allows the user to conditionally schedule management activities such as harvests and natural disturbances, based on a set of conditions that must occur or thresholds that must be reached. The event monitor contains predefined variables but also allows the creation of custom variables. Some predefined variables are tied to specific FVS extensions. The predicted fisher resting habitat value is estimated via a predefined FFE event monitor variable, which we call FISHERIN (calculated using the variables and coefficients in the parametric version of the model [Zielinski et. al. 2006]). The initial step involves activating the FFE (using the keywords FMIN and END), so that snag information is being tracked. The FVS can then calculate the predicted probability of resting habitat value, both before and after each harvest, vegetation treatment, or disturbance using a COMPUTE – END event monitor sequence.

As a demonstration of how one would use FVS to evaluate the effects of various treatments on predicted fisher resting value, we chose data from nine plots in five forest stands in the Sierra National Forest. These data were collected in support of an unrelated project, utilizing typical stand exam procedures. Plots were chosen with the goal of including a range of likely predicted fisher resting habitat values such that there were three plots each with low, medium, and high predicted fisher resting habitat value. For these plots, the value for the slope variable was derived from the stand the plot occurred in, and was not measured at the level of the plot. Each plot was subjected to a control (untreated but allowing for growth) and three simulated treatments in FVS: thin from below with a 12-in (30.5-cm) maximum diameter limit and a minimum of 60 percent canopy cover retained (12-in & 60%), thin from below with a 30-in (76.2-cm) maximum dbh limit and a minimum of 50 percent canopy cover retained (30-in & 50%), and thin from below with a 40-in (101.6-cm) maximum diameter limit and a minimum of 35 percent canopy cover retained (40-in & 35%). Trees that were < 4 in (10.2 cm) dbh at the time of simulated harvest were not removed, because there is typically no market for them. The three thinning scenarios, varying along a harvest tree size and canopy cover continuum, were applied (via simulation) to the plots in their current (2009) status. Predicted fisher resting habitat value was estimated in 2009, the simulated treatments occurred, and resting habitat value was estimated again at 5-year intervals into the future: 2014, 2019, and 2024. We predicted fisher resting habitat value for each year represented by the mean and standard error, calculated for the three plots in each initial predicted category (low, moderate, and high). Stand visualization software (SVS) (McGaughey 1997; http:forsys.cfr.washington.edu/svs.html) was used to portray the composition of each plot at each time step. The simulations we chose were not intended to evaluate specific prescriptions that were being considered by forest managers on the Sierra National Forest; rather they were simply an example of the range of typical prescriptions that are available to managers of mixed-conifer forests on the west side of the Sierra Nevada.

Results

Preliminary Analyses: Addressing Changes in the FIA Protocol

The plot-aggregated values of the predictor variables were strongly correlated when comparing the old protocol and the new protocol (r = 0.65 to 0.89), except for dominant canopy cover (r = 0.32). The predicted fisher resting habitat value, when calculated based on variables collected by the old and new FIA protocol, was more strongly correlated using the parametric version of the model (r = 0.66) than the nonparametric version (r = 0.56). Some differences in values from the same plot were expected because the subplots of each design were located in different places, some different trees were sampled, and some samples were collected several years apart. Sierran forests may be particularly patchy (more spatially variable) compared to other forests (e.g., North et al. 2004), resulting in greater differences between plot designs than might be expected in other forests. Nevertheless, the similarity in the means and standard deviations for most attributes and the resting site probabilities (table 1) suggests there were no substantial effects of plot design on the distribution of values calculated. The exception was the calculation of dominant canopy cover, which may have resulted from differences in how crews were instructed to code tree dominance (e.g., by layer height vs. by light exposure). Nonetheless, the similarity in mean predicted fisher resting site probability among plot protocols for the nonparametric model (0.156 vs. 0.165) suggests the effect of differences in canopy cover calculation was not substantial.

Preliminary Analyses: Estimating the Predicted Resting Habitat Variables in FVS

The differences between the estimates for each variable **calculated** from the FIA data versus those **generated** in FVS were generally small, are distributed about zero, and average very close to zero (table 2). The FVS approximation for percentage canopy cover is the most error-prone of the variables (table 2). Although the calculated values for predicted resting habitat may not be identical when compared to those generated from the FIA data, they are close and useful as an index of the predicted value for the purpose of comparing management alternatives.

Table 1—Mean and standard deviation of predictor variables and parametric and nonparametric fisher resting site probabilities for 69 undisturbed, fully forested plots in the study area measured with the periodic protocol and remeasured with the annual protocol (see text for protocol differences) within 2 to 8 years (mean = 4.7 years)

	Periodic		Annual	
	Mean	Standard deviation	Mean	Standard deviation
DBH_MAX	104.7	43.9	102.6	42.8
BA_S	14.0	9.9	14.8	9.3
SLOPE	37.7	17.6	36.2	16.2
CC	41.5	21.3	49.5	25.7
CONSNG	75.9	51.4	72.1	54.5
DBH_HWD	10.6	13.4	9.0	11.4
Predicted resting habitat value:				
Parametric	0.147	0.143	0.158	0.167
Nonparametric	0.156	0.187	0.165	0.205

DBH_MAX = maximum tree diameter at breast height (dbh), BA_S = basal area of trees ≤ 51 cm dbh, SLOPE = percentage of slope, CC = overstory tree canopy cover, CONSNG = dbh of largest conifer snag, DBH_HWD = average hardwood dbh.

Table 2—Values of the predictors from the fisher resting habitat model from five plots in the Sierra Nevada, calculated either directly from the Forest Inventory and Analysis (FIA) data or calculated using the Forest Vegetation Simulator (FVS) software

	DBH_MAX		BA_S		SLOPE		CC		CONSNG		DBH_HWD		Predicted resting habitat value		
Plot	FIA	FVS	FIA	FVS	FIA	FVS	FIA	FVS	FIA	FVS	FIA	FVS	FIA	FVS	Difference
5630	58.42	58.42	3.94	3.94	48.75	48.75	29.94	33.08	0	0	20.72	20.72	0.010	0.008	0.0018
6312	67.82	67.82	3.00	3.00	33.75	33.75	41.93	41.93	90.93	90.93	3.92	3.92	0.017	0.011	0.0055
5534	98.04	98.04	21.15	21.15	26.25	26.25	97.56	159.72	85.34	85.34	13.11	13.11	0.288	0.377	0.0889
8994	125.22	125.22	18.49	18.49	45.00	45.00	130.11	185.78	21.59	21.59	7.23	7.23	0.409	0.473	0.0641
6786	139.45	139.45	16.34	16.34	38.75	38.75	83.73	55.13	131.83	125.60	41.87	41.87	0.585	0.435	0.1506

DBH_MAX = maximum tree diameter at breast height (dbh), BA_S = basal area of trees ≤ 51 cm dbh, SLOPE = percentage of slope, CC = overstory tree canopy cover, CONSNG = dbh of largest conifer snag, DBH_HWD = average hardwood dbh.
Source: Zielinski et al. (2006).

Monitoring Status and Change of Predicted Resting Habitat

The means (and standard deviations) of predicted fisher resting habitat value for 1997 and 2004 were 0.146 (0.008) and 0.135 (0.010), respectively (fig. 2; "All four national forests"). Estimated values for individual national forests (NF) differed in the direction of change between the 1997 and 2004 samples (fig. 2). Disturbance codes recorded on the plots suggest that recent harvest or fire on 20 percent of the plots measured on Eldorado NF may be responsible for the decline in predicted habitat, caused by declines in basal area of trees < 51 cm dbh, canopy cover, dbh of the largest conifer snag, and average hardwood dbh. Despite recent fire recorded on 17 percent of the Sequoia NF plots, predicted habitat increased, apparently caused by much higher canopy cover values recorded in 2004. Predicted values on private

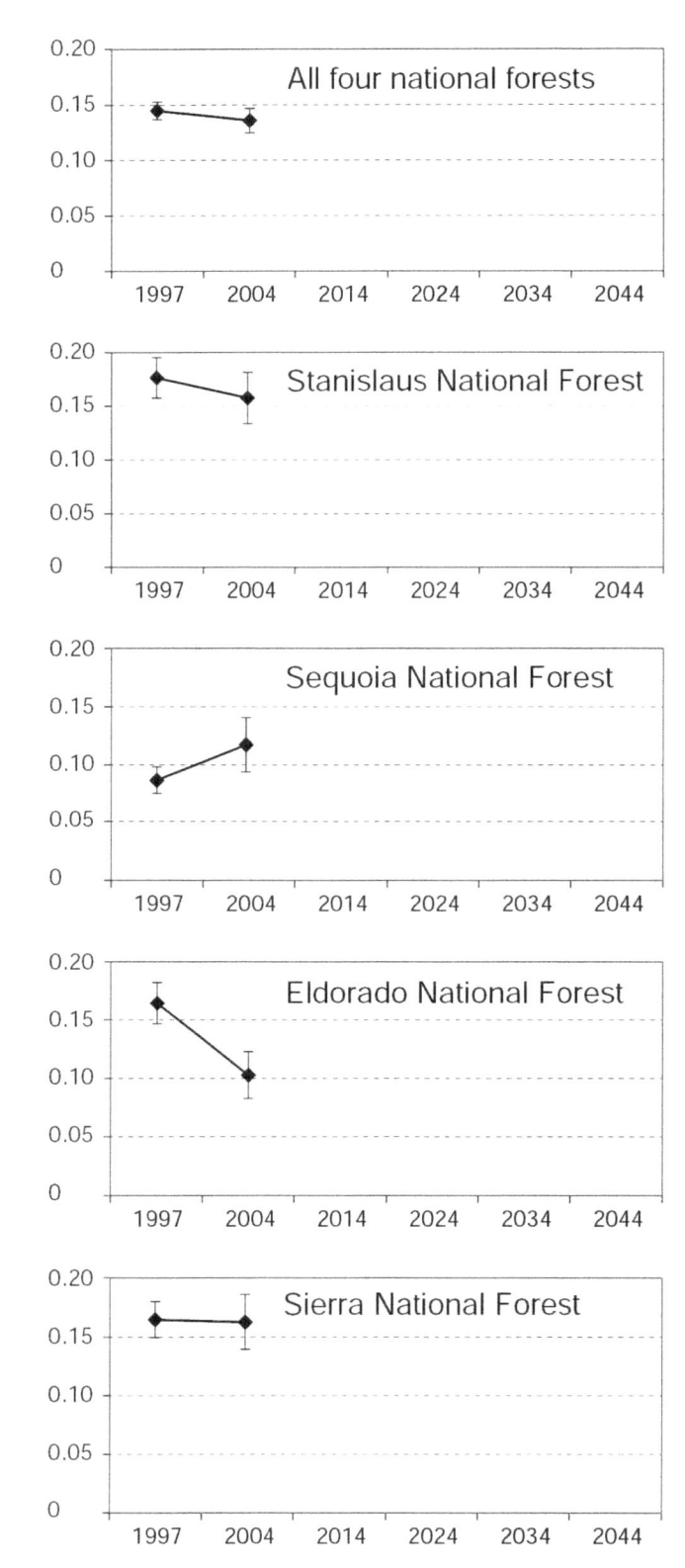

Figure 2—Estimates of predicted fisher resting habitat value at 1997 and 2004 for each of the four southern Sierra Nevada national forests and for all four collectively. Bars are standard errors. The years 2014, 2024, and beyond are included to illustrate the opportunities for monitoring trend in predicted resting habitat value when future vegetation data become available. Sample sizes (N) are as follows, for 1997 and 2004, respectively: All four national forests = 626, 283; Stanislaus National Forest = 139, 61; Sequoia National Forest = 196, 92; Eldorado National Forest = 128, 60; and Sierra National Forest = 163, 70.

lands were lower, in general, than on federal or state lands (mean [SE] 2007 predicted resting value private = 0.076 [0.02] and USFS land = 0.135 [0.011]). However, there is little private land within the specified elevations in the vicinity of the four national forests in the southern Sierra Nevada, resulting in fewer of the plots occurring on private lands (15.2 percent). This may account for the larger standard error (especially relative to the mean) of predicted resting habitat value on private lands.

Simulating the Effects of Silvicultural Alternatives

In our example, FVS simulated the effect of treatments over 15 years at nine plots that differed considerably in their initial predicted value to fishers as resting habitat (fig. 3). Plots with the highest initial predicted suitability (bottom row, fig. 4) had greater canopy cover, greater variation in tree size, and more hardwood and large snag components than those with much lower predicted values (top row, fig. 4). Not surprisingly, the magnitude of treatment effects was greatest for plots that began with

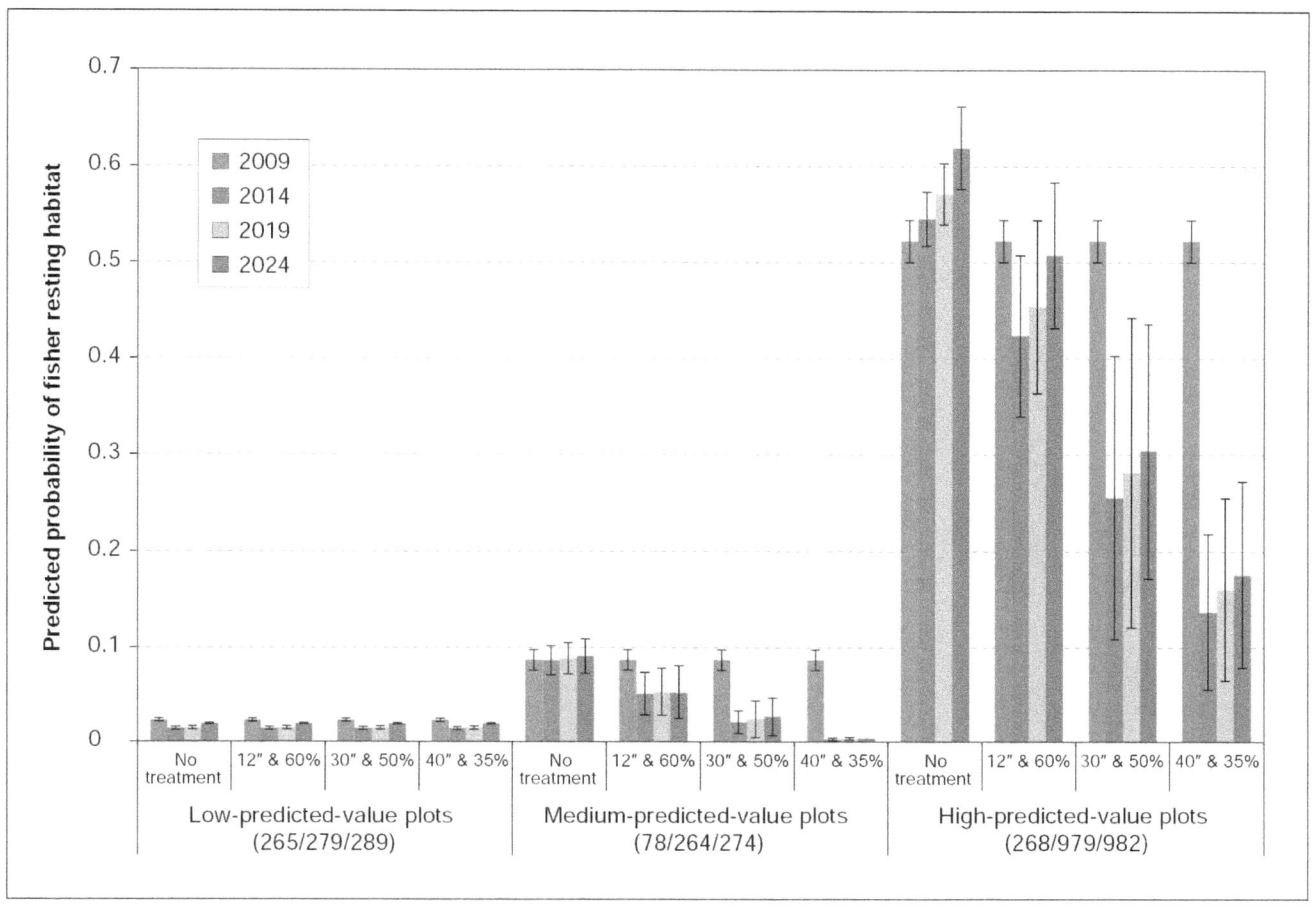

Figure 3—Estimates of predicted fisher resting habitat value on the Sierra National Forest as a function of a control and three treatments simulated in the Forest Vegetation Simulator: (1) thinning to a 12-in (30.5-cm) dbh maximum and down to 60 percent canopy cover (12-in & 60%), (2) thinning to a 30-in (76.2-cm) dbh maximum and down to 50 percent canopy cover (30-in & 50%), and (3) thinning to a 40-in (101.6-cm) dbh maximum and down to 35 percent canopy cover (40-in & 35%). FVS assessed the predicted resting habitat value in 2009 and at 5-year intervals until 2024. N = 3 replicate plots for each combination of treatment and class of initial predicted value (low, medium, and high); bars are standard errors.

the highest predicted values (fig. 3). Plots with high initial value had more habitat value to lose when treatments removed larger trees and reduced residual canopy cover. Owing to the short timeframe of our evaluation, plots with low predicted initial value could only change moderately under even the most ideal growing conditions. The mean of the plots with the highest initial resting habitat values dropped proportionately when the simulated treatments removed trees of increasing minimum size and decreasing residual canopy cover. This decrease is conspicuous when the future status (in year 2024) of two of the plots with initially high predicted resting habitat value (plots 979 and 982) are represented using stand visualization imagery (fig. 5).

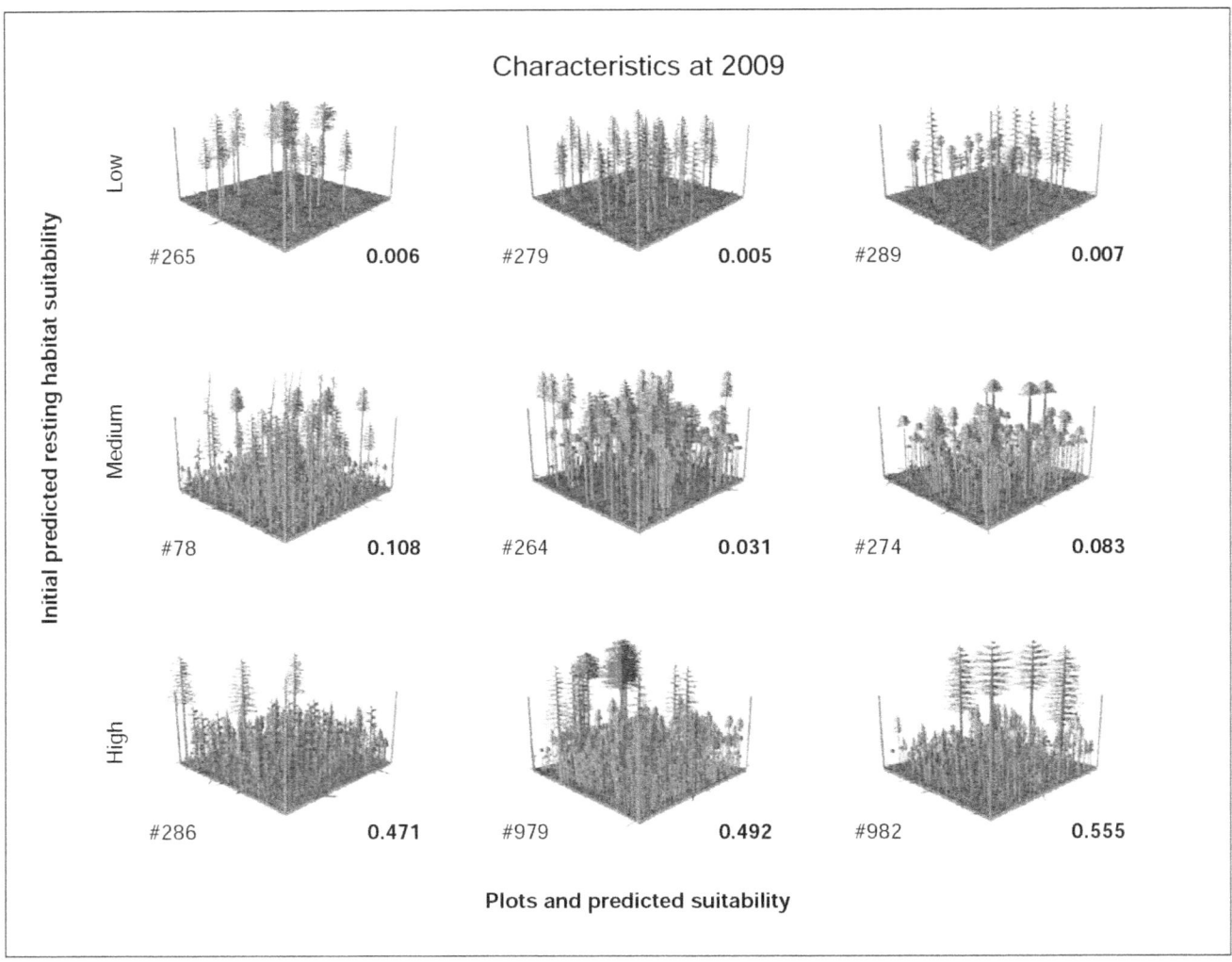

Figure 4—Stand visualization system images of the **current state** (2009) of nine plots on the Sierra National Forest described in the Forest Vegetation Simulator. The plots were chosen to include three plots with low, medium, and high predicted resting habitat value. Predicted resting habitat value is noted in lower right corner of each image.

In general, predicted resting habitat value decreased proportional to severity of thinning (and the decrease in canopy cover). The fact that control plots increased in predicted habitat value over time (fig. 3) suggested that the simulations were performing logically. Interestingly, high-value plots having the lightest thinning (12-in & 60%) returned to their pretreatment habitat value within the 15-year simulation horizon (fig. 3).

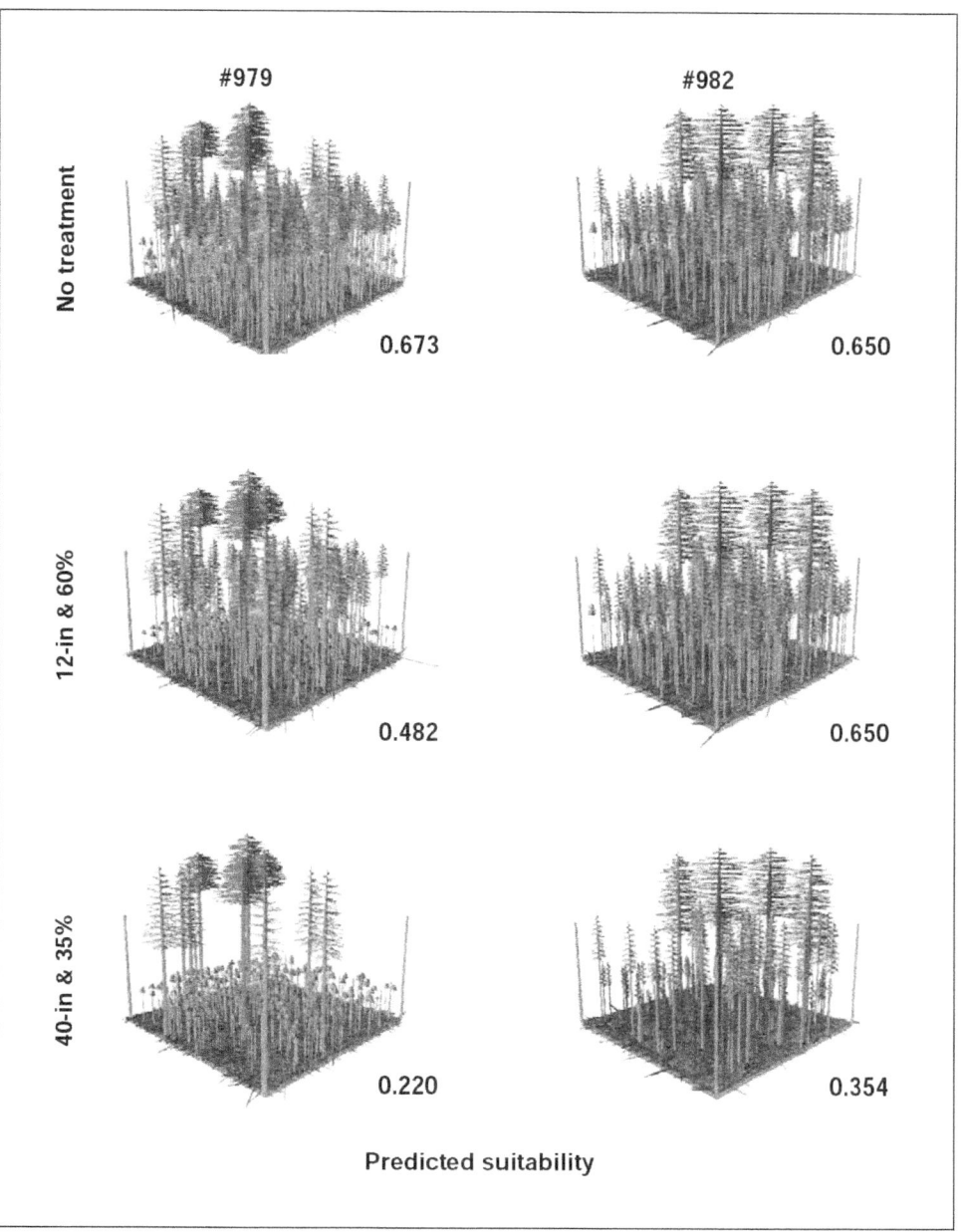

Figure 5—Stand visualization system images of the **future simulated state** (2024) of two plots (numbers 979 and 982) on the Sierra National Forest that started with relatively high predicted fisher resting habitat value. The 2024 condition is simulated for three conditions: (1) no treatment, (2) thinning to a 12-in (30.5-cm) dbh maximum and down to 60 percent canopy cover (12-in and 60%) and thinning to a 40-in (101.6-cm) dbh maximum and down to 35 percent canopy cover (40-in and 35%). The number of small trees that are present after the thinning treatments represent those that were smaller than the 4-in (10.2-cm) minimum 15 years earlier, at the time of simulated harvest (see "Methods"). Predicted resting habitat value is noted in lower right corner of each image.

Discussion

We demonstrated that an empirically derived habitat model, created using the FIA vegetation sampling protocol and implemented in FVS, is capable of producing quantitative measures of the status and trend in predicted fisher resting habitat value and is useful for evaluating the effects of simulated vegetation treatments. This is a major step toward developing methods to analyze the effects of forest management and change on important microhabitat features for a sensitive forest-dependent species. Our approach can facilitate a number of quantitative comparisons (see fig. 1), including monitoring change in predicted value over time and comparing predicted value among lands under different ownership and management. We have also demonstrated that the FIA-based model performs well in FVS, which means that predicted fisher resting value can be yet another output from analyses that compare the effects of silvicultural treatments on vegetation structure and composition, timber volume, and the abundance of fuels, among other traditional outputs. Such comparisons also provide a more refined and quantitative approach to evaluating land management scenarios relative to their potential impacts on habitat of threatened, endangered, or sensitive species.

Prior to the availability of this tool, most public land managers were using crude, expert-opinion-based systems, such as California Wildlife Habitat Relations (CWHR) system (Mayer and Laudenslayer 1988), to estimate the effects of various treatments on fisher habitat. When not using these very general models, land managers often applied the results of research on fishers conducted at nearby small study areas, typically at scales that are inappropriate. In other words, they did the best they could, given the quality and quantity of information available. An exception is a similarly quantitative tool, which we are developing and testing in cooperation with managers on the Sierra National Forest. This new project uses FVS to understand how the simulated results of **landscape-level** treatments differ from the characteristics of home ranges chosen by female fishers.[2] This work will provide, for the home range scale, a tool similar to that developed here at the scale of the resting site.

The approach we used, of building models with FIA-based predictors, can be applied to other species provided that researchers plan, from the beginning of their work, to measure FIA-based variables at locations of importance to the species of interest. For example, we have used FIA plot data to predict the

---

[2] Thompson, C.M.; Zielinski, W.J.; Purcell, K.L. The use of landscape trajectory analysis to evaluate management risks: a case study with the fisher in the Sierra National Forest. On file with: W.J. Zielinski, Arcata, CA.

occurrence of terrestrial salamanders, mollusks, and rodents (Dunk and Hawley 2009, Dunk et al. 2004, Welsh et al. 2006). For these small vertebrates and invertebrates, one can build a model to actually predict occurrence (or even abundance) of the species on existing plots within the FIA annual inventory system, provided that the plot can be sampled without disturbance. Although the models constructed for these small species were developed using FIA plot data, they have not been vetted through the FVS system and thus require more examination before they can be used for the various purposes proposed here for the fisher model (see fig. 1). It would not be difficult, however, to prepare them for this purpose.

The approach for species that use larger areas must be different. As demonstrated here for the fisher, and for other species that use areas that are much larger than the typical 1-ha FIA plot footprint, models must be constructed by installing new FIA plots **centered on a habitat element of conservation importance** (e.g., a resting, denning, roosting, or nesting site) or distributed at relatively high density within forest stands of particular importance to the species. For these larger species, the plots installed for this purpose are off the regular FIA grid and intended to be sampled only once, for the specific purpose of developing the predictive habitat model. As demonstrated here for the fisher, this model can then be used to predict habitat value at the routinely resampled FIA vegetation plots that fall within the region of inference each time they are resampled. A useful habitat model constructed in this fashion can be applied to subsequently sampled data at FIA plots in perpetuity, or until the relationship between the species and its habitat changes. If this happens, a new habitat relationship model, based on new empirical FIA-based field data, would need to be developed.

The FIA-based wildlife habitat models can reveal important contrasts in the predicted value of lands managed for different purposes. For example, Huff et al. (2006) used FIA-based sampling to estimate the area of high suitability nesting habitat for marbled murrelets and contrasted values for each of the Pacific States. Dunk and Hawley (2009) used FIA-based sampling to evaluate habitat and reserve associations of the red tree vole (*Arborimus longicaudus*) throughout the majority of the species' range. Subsequently, their model was used to evaluate the distribution of suitable tree vole habitat within various land ownership categories (using FIA data) within a smaller portion of the species' range, in order to assist in the evaluation of a petition to list the red tree vole under the Endangered Species Act (J. Dunk. 2009. Personal communication, Department of Environmental Science and Management, Humboldt State University, Arcata, CA). As demonstrated here, predicted values from our model can be used in a similar fashion, to contrast resting habitat value among national forests and between public and private lands. Moreover, if we assumed a threshold predicted value, above which sites are assumed to be "resting habitat," our model could also be used (sensu Huff et al. 2006) to estimate the amount and distribution of resting habitat.

Every predictive habitat model has spatial boundaries. The model we have developed applies only to the area over which we collected the resting site data from radio-collared fishers, which includes relevant elevations on the west slope of the Sierra and Sequoia National Forests. Applications for other portions of the fisher's range will require the development of separate models. We are in the process of doing this to predict resting habitat in northwestern California, and we expect that the variables in the selected model will be quite different than those that appear in the model used here. This has already been confirmed in habitat selection work that was developed outside the FIA framework; variables that predicted fisher resting sites in the southern Sierra Nevada were different than those that predicted resting sites in northwestern California (Zielinski et al. 2004). Thus, we caution against applying the current model outside the southern Sierra Nevada.

During the course of developing the model for the southern Sierra Nevada, we learned that we could probably improve future applications for fishers, and for other species, in terms of how two of the variables were estimated from FIA data or interpreted in FVS: canopy cover and slope. The derivation of canopy cover was indirect and awkward in FVS, requiring information from the FIA plot data about the dominance status (predominant, dominant, or codominant) and crown ratio, by species, for all trees > 1 in dbh. We believe that the estimation of canopy cover would be easier to generate, and less variable, if it excluded consideration of dominance status and was based instead simply on total tree cover. Percentage of slope, in developing the original fisher model, was estimated at each plot. However, when the model is applied to new plots, which may not have been measured using the FIA protocol, slope may not have been measured at the plot, only at the level of the stand. This was the situation for the test data evaluated in our examples (figs. 3 through 5). When measured this way, all plots that occur within the same stand will have the same value for slope, regardless of the true slope at the plot. Given how influential the slope variable is in estimating the predicted resting habitat value (Zielinski et al. 2006), this can result in an application of the model that predicts resting habitat value with less precision. We suggest that as practitioners plan to use this model, they should use slope data measured specifically for each plot.

Forest planning is an increasingly complex process in which the stakeholders demand a rigorous and scientific approach. Linking our description of fisher resting habitat to FIA and FVS fulfills the need for quantitative predictions of the effects of forest management scenarios. Land managers are not served well by the research community when we do not provide tools that are useable to them. Without such tools, managers will continue to use literature reviews, results from small-scale studies, general habitat models (e.g., CWHR models; California Department of Fish and Game 1992), or their professional opinion to evaluate the effects of proposed management actions. The various publics that scrutinize land management planning documents are sophisticated and call for increasingly more exacting standards to evaluate the effects of proposed actions on species and their habitat. Our approach fulfills that need for analyses of fisher resting habitat that occur in the southern Sierra Nevada.

Successful application of a wildlife habitat model that is integrated with institutional forest monitoring and prediction requires considerable effort. This work cannot be done by a wildlife biologist in isolation. It requires front-end co-development with specialists familiar with the inventory, monitoring, and forest simulation technologies that will be used to describe the effects on the target species. Research must be designed for **application**, in much the same way an experiment is designed, a priori, to be **statistically** valid. We describe here the process of translating research results into a quantitative tool for decisionmakers. The fisher provides one example of how habitat assessments for other species of wildlife could be advanced if they were developed together with managers, in a language familiar to managers, and with their implementation success as a goal.

Acknowledgments

We thank T. Gaman of East-West Forestry for contributions to the development of the original fisher FIA model and for collecting FIA plot data necessary to construct the original model. R. Schlexer helped manage the FIA plot data. We are grateful to E. Smith-Mateja, C. Keyser, K. Purcell, and W. Spencer for review comments and R. Schlexer and L. Sullivan for editorial assistance. Funding for the development of the FIA-based fisher model was contributed by the Pacific Southwest Region of the USDA Forest Service and the Yreka office of the USDI Fish and Wildlife Service.

English Equivalents

When you know:	Multiply by:	To find:
Centimeters (cm)	0.394	Inches (in)
Meters (m)	3.28	Feet (ft)
Kilometers (km)	.621	Miles (mi)
Square kilometers (km^2)	.386	Square miles (mi^2)
Hectares (ha)	2.47	Acres

Literature Cited

Bailey, R.G. 1994. Descriptions of the ecoregions of the United States. 2nd ed. Misc. Publ. 1391 (revised). Washington, DC: U.S. Department of Agriculture, Forest Service. 108 p.

Bechtold, W.A.; Patterson, P.L., eds. 2004. The enhanced Forest Inventory and Analysis Program—national sampling design and estimation procedures. Gen. Tech. Rep. SRS-80. Asheville, NC: U.S. Department of Agriculture, Forest Service, Southern Research Station. 85 p.

Burnham, K.P.; Anderson, D.R. 2002. Model selection and multi-model inference: a practical information-theoretic approach. 2nd ed. New York: Springer-Verlag. 488 p.

California Department of Fish and Game. 1992. CWHR version 8.0 personal computer program. Sacramento, CA: California Interagency Wildlife Task Group.

Christensen, G.; Campbell, S.J.; Fried, J.S. 2008. California's forest resources, 2001–2005: five-year Forest Inventory and Analysis report. PNW-GTR-763. Portland, OR: U.S. Department of Agriculture, Forest Service, Pacific Northwest Research Station. 183 p.

Dixon, G.E., comp. 2003. Essential FVS: a user's guide to the Forest Vegetation Simulator. Internal Rep. Fort Collins, CO: U.S. Department of Agriculture, Forest Service, Forest Management Service Center. 193 p.

Dunk, J.R.; Hawley, J.J.V.G. 2009. Red-tree vole habitat suitability modeling: implications for conservation and management. Forest Ecology and Management. 258: 626–634.

Dunk, J.R.; Zielinski, W.J.; Preisler, H.K. 2004. Predicting the occurrence of rare mollusks in northern California forests. Ecological Applications. 14: 713–729.

Fearer, T.M.; Prisley, S.P.; Stauffer, D.F.; Keyser, P.D. 2007. A method for integrating the Breeding Bird Survey and Forest Inventory and Analysis databases to evaluate forest bird-habitat relationships at multiple scales. Forest Ecology and Management. 243: 128–143.

Hastie, T.J.; Tibshirani, R.J. 1990. Generalized additive models. New York: Chapman and Hall. 356 p.

Huff, M.H.; Raphael, M.G.; Miller, S.L.; Nelson, S.K.; Baldwin, J., tech. coords. 2006. Northwest Forest Plan—the first 10 years (1994–2003): status and trends of population and nesting habitat for the marbled murrelet. Gen. Tech. Rep. PNW-GTR-650. Portland, OR: U.S. Department of Agriculture, Forest Service, Pacific Northwest Research Station. 149 p.

Jennings, S.B.; Brown, N.D.; Sheil, D. 1999. Assessing forest canopies and understorey illumination: canopy closure, canopy cover and other measures. Forestry. 72: 59–77.

Larson, M.A.; Thompson, F.R., III; Millspaugh, J.J.; Dijak, W.D.; Shifley, S.R. 2004. Linking population viability, habitat suitability, and landscape simulation models for conservation planning. Ecological Modeling. 180: 103–118.

Mayer, K.E.; Laudenslayer, W.F., Jr. 1988. A guide to the wildlife habitats of California. California Department of Forestry and Fire Protection, Sacramento. 166 p.

Mazzoni, A.K. 2002. Habitat use by fishers (*Martes pennanti*) in the southern Sierra Nevada, California. Fresno, CA: California State University. 96 p. M.S. thesis.

McDermid, G.J.; Hall, R.J.; Sanchez-Azofeifa, G.A.; Franklin, S.E.; Stenhouse, G.B.; Tobliuk, T.; LeDrew, E.F. 2009. Remote sensing and forest inventory for wildlife habitat assessment. Forest Ecology and Management. 257: 2262–2269.

McGaughey, R.J. 1997. Visualizing forest stand dynamics using the stand visualization system. In: Proceedings, 1997 ASPRS-ACSM-RTI spring convention. Bethesda, MD: American Congress on Surveying and Mapping. 4: 248–257.

Nichols, J.D.; Williams, B.K. 2006. Monitoring for conservation. Trends in Ecology and Evolution. 21: 668–673.

North, M.; Chen, J.; Oakley, B.; Song, B.; Rudnicki, M.; Gray, A.; Innes, J. 2004. Forest stand structure and pattern of old-growth western hemlock/Douglas-fir and mixed-conifer forests. Forest Science. 50: 299–311.

Reinhardt, E.D.; Crookston, N.L.; Rebain, S.A., tech. eds. 2007. The fire and fuels extension to the Forest Vegetation Simulator. Addendum to Gen. Tech. Rep. RMRS-GTR-116. Ogden, UT: U.S. Department of Agriculture, Forest Service, Rocky Mountain Research Station. 208 p.

Slauson, K.M.; Zielinski, W.J.; Hayes, J.P. 2007. Habitat selection by American martens in coastal California. Journal of Wildlife Management. 71: 459–468.

Spies, T.A.; McComb, B.C.; Kennedy, R.; McGrath, M.T.; Olsen, K.; Pabst, R.J. 2007. Potential effects of forest policies on terrestrial biodiversity in a multi-ownership province. Ecological Applications. 17: 48–65.

U.S. Department of Agriculture, Forest Service. 2007. Forest Inventory and Analysis national core field guide. Volume I: Field data collection procedures for phase 2 plots, Version 4.0. Washington, DC: U.S. Department of Agriculture, Forest Service. 203 p.

Vallecillo, S.; Brotons, L.; Thuiller, W. 2009. Dangers of predicting bird species distributions in response to land-cover changes. Ecological Applications. 19: 538–549.

Warbington, R.W.; Levitan, J. 1992. How to estimate canopy cover using maximum crown width/dbh relationships. In: Lund, G.; Landis, E.; Atterbury, T., eds. Proceedings, stand inventory technologies '92: an international multiple resource conference. Bethesda, MD: American Society for Photogrammetry and Remote Sensing: 319–328.

Welsh, H.H., Jr.; Dunk, J.R.; Zielinski; W.J. 2006. Developing and applying habitat models using forest inventory data: an example using a terrestrial salamander. Journal of Wildlife Management. 70: 671–681.

Wycoff, W.R.; Crookston, N.L.; Stage, A.R. 1982. User's guide to the stand prognosis model. Gen. Tech. Rep. INT-133. Ogden, UT: U.S. Department of Agriculture, Forest Service, Intermountain Forest and Range Experiment Station. 112 p.

Yoccoz, N.G.; Nichols, J.D.; Boulinier, T. 2001. Monitoring of biological diversity in space and time. Trends in Ecology and Evolution. 16: 446–453.

Zielinski, W.J.; Truex, R.L.; Dunk, J.R.; Gaman, T. 2006. Using forest inventory data to assess fisher resting habitat suitability in California. Ecological Applications. 16(3): 1010–1025.

Zielinski, W.J.; Truex, R.L.; Ogan, C.; Busse, K. 1997. Detection surveys for fishers and American martens in California, 1989–1994: summary and interpretations. In: Proulx, G.; Bryant, H.N.; Woodard, P.M., eds. *Martes*: taxonomy, ecology, techniques, and management. Edmonton, AB: The Provincial Museum of Alberta: 372–392.

Zielinski, W.J.; Truex, R.L.; Schmidt, G.A.; Schlexer, F.V.; Schmidt, K.N.; Barrett, R.H. 2004. Resting habitat selection by fishers in California. Journal of Wildlife Management. 68: 475–492.

Appendix A

A-1: Example keyword file needed to run the Forest Vegetation Simulator.

This hypothetical example shows the commands needed to simulate a thinning scenario. The existing stand is thinned to maintain approximately 60 percent of the stand basal area. The predicted fisher resting site value (hereafter the "Fisher index") is tracked throughout the simulation. Lines beginning with the "*" character are treated as comment lines by FVS and are useful for documentation. Additional information available in Dixon 2003.

```
*----------

* This section of keywords gives control instructions to FVS.
* It's telling FVS what stand has been selected, the stand's
* inventory year, to run 6 projection cycles, with the first
* cycle 7 years long rather than the default 10 years. The
* database keywords tell FVS how to select the stand and
* tree data from the ACCESS Database.

*----------

*
Screen
StandCN
647B
InvYear         2003
TimeInt             1           7
NumCycle            6
*
Database
DSNIn
snfplus04_1inv.mdb
StandSQL
SELECT *
FROM FVS_StandInit
WHERE Stand_CN = '%Stand_CN%'
EndSQL
TreeSQL
SELECT *
FROM FVS_TreeInit
WHERE Stand_CN = '%Stand_CN%'
EndSQL
END
*----------
* This section of keywords instructs FVS to simulate a thinning.
* In this example, it only thins trees greater than 1" DBH and
* less than 25" DBH.
*----------
```

```
*
ThinDBH          2010         1        25       1.      All       0.        41
*
*----------
* This section of keywords initiates the Fire and Fuels extension of FVS
* which is needed to provide snag information for the calculation of the
* Fisher index. It also instructs FVS to compute two user-defined Fisher
* index values, BFI and AFI, defined as follows:
*     BFI is the Fisher index value at the start of each projection cycle;
*     AFI is the Fisher index value after a cutting occurs, and is computed
*     whenever a thinning occurs in the simulation.
*----------
*
FMIN
END
*
COMPUTE          0
BFI = FISHERIN
END
IF
EVPHASE EQ 2 AND CUT EQ 1
THEN
COMPUTE
AFI = FISHERIN
END
ENDIF
*
*----------
*----------
* This section instructs FVS to send the computed variables (described above)
* and the stand summary data to an EXCEL file.
*----------
DataBase
DSNOut
FVSout.xls
Summary
Compute          0          0
End
*----------
* These are FVS control keywords telling the model to start the
* simulation and stop when it is done. FVS has the ability to simulate
* several management scenarios within one run sequence.
*----------
*
PROCESS
STOP
```

A-2: Example output showing how FVS can send the computed variables and stand summary statistics to an output format. As requested in the keyword file, the variable BFI (the Fisher Index value at the start of each projection cycle) is displayed for every projection cycle, and the variable AFI (the Fisher Index value after a treatment or disturbance occurs) is only displayed after a harvest cut in a projection cycle. a = example output in original database format; b = output in Excel format.

a:

Id	CaseID	StandID	Year	BFI	AFI
1	1	647B	2003	0.4832	
2	1	647B	2010	0.5441	0.1232
3	1	647B	2020	0.1886	
4	1	647B	2030	0.2685	
5	1	647B	2040	0.2980	
6	1	647B	2050	0.3555	

Id	CaseID	StandID	Year	Age	Tpa	BA	SDI
1	1	647B	2003	0	660	197	406
2	1	647B	2010	7	640	211	427
3	1	647B	2020	17	667	153	332
4	1	647B	2030	27	661	178	375
5	1	647B	2040	37	632	197	403
6	1	647B	2050	47	596	215	428
7	1	647B	2060	57	571	236	458

b:

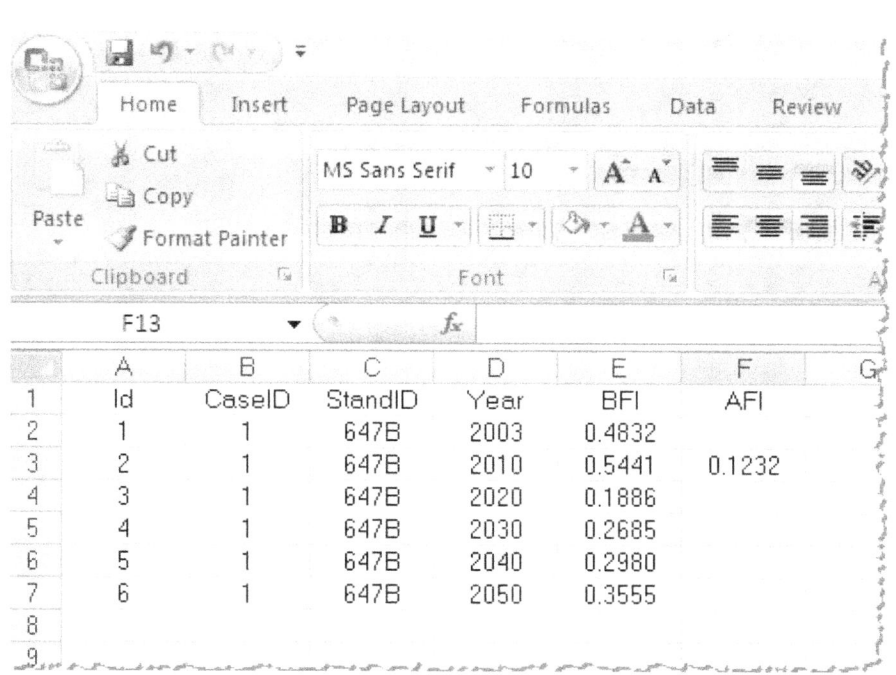

	A	B	C	D	E	F	G
1	Id	CaseID	StandID	Year	BFI	AFI	
2	1	1	647B	2003	0.4832		
3	2	1	647B	2010	0.5441	0.1232	
4	3	1	647B	2020	0.1886		
5	4	1	647B	2030	0.2685		
6	5	1	647B	2040	0.2980		
7	6	1	647B	2050	0.3555		
8							
9							

	A	B	C	D	E	F	G	H
1	Id	CaseID	StandID	Year	Age	Tpa	BA	SDI
2	1	1	647B	2003	0	660	197	406
3	2	1	647B	2010	7	640	211	427
4	3	1	647B	2020	17	667	153	332
5	4	1	647B	2030	27	661	178	375
6	5	1	647B	2040	37	632	197	403
7	6	1	647B	2050	47	596	215	428
8	7	1	647B	2060	57	571	236	458

A-3: Fortran computer code listing for the FVS subroutine that computes the Fisher Index.

```
      ENTRY FISHER (FINDX)
C----------
C  THIS ENTRY COMPUTES A VALUE FOR THE FISHER RESTING HABITAT
C  SUITABILITY (THE "FISHER INDEX")
C
C  REF: ZIELINSKI, WILLIAM J.; TRUEX, RICHARD L.; DUNK, JEFFREY R.;
C       GAMAN, TOM. 2006. USING FOREST INVENTORY DATA TO ASSESS FISHER
C       RESTING HABITAT SUITABILITY IN CALIFORNIA. ECOLOGICAL
C       APPLICATIONS 16(3). PP 1010-1025.
C----------
C  SEE IF WE NEED TO DO SOME DEBUG.
C----------
      CALL DBCHK (DEBUG,'FISHER',6,ICYC)
      IF(DEBUG)WRITE(JOSTND,10)ICYC
   10 FORMAT(' ENTERING SUBROUTINE EVPDEF, ENTRY FISHER, CYCLE =',I4)
C----------
C  INITIALIZE VARIABLES.
C----------
      TEMP = 0.
      FINDX = 0.
      BASM = 0.
      CCPCT = 0.
      ADHW = 0.
      DMAX = 0.
      DSNMAX = 0.
C----------
C  IF FIRE MODEL IS NOT ACTIVE, FOR SNAG PROCESSING, RETURN A ZERO.
C----------
      CALL FMATV(LFIRE2)
      IF(.NOT. LFIRE2)GO TO 500
C----------
C  THIS IS CURRENTLY ONLY ALLOWED IN THE CALIFORNIA VARIANTS AND
C  ONLY FOR R5 FORESTS (I.E. BASED ON R5 CROWN WIDTH EQNS).
C----------
      CALL VARVER(VVER)
      IF(VVER(:2).EQ.'NC' .AND. IFOR.NE.4 .AND. IFOR.NE.5)THEN
        GO TO 20
      ELSEIF(VVER(:2).EQ.'CA' .AND. IFOR.LT.6)THEN
        GO TO 20
      ELSEIF(VVER(:2).EQ.'SO' .AND. IFOR.GT.3)THEN
        GO TO 20
      ELSEIF(VVER(:2).EQ.'WS')THEN
        GO TO 20
      ELSE
        GO TO 500
      ENDIF
   20 CONTINUE
      IF(ITRN .LE. 0) GO TO 500
```

```
C----------
C  CANOPY COVER PERCENT IS ONLY FOR PREDOMINANT, DOMINANT, AND
CODOMINENT
C  TREES. PROXY THIS BY TAKING ALL TREES WHICH ARE AT LEAST AS TALL
AS
C  50% OF THE HEIGHT OF THE 90TH %-TILE TREE IN THE HEIGHT
DISTRIBUTION
C
C  EXCLUDE TREES WITH CROWN RATIO LESS THAN 30% FROM THE CALCULATION.
C  EXCLUDE TREES WITH DBH LT 1" FROM THE CALCULATION
C  FIRST SORT BY HT. NEXT LOOP THROUGH THE TREES AND COMPUTE PERCENT
C  CANOPY COVER.
C----------
      DO 25 I=1,MAXTRE
      IF(I .LE. ITRN)THEN
        INDEX(I)=I
      ELSE
        INDEX(I)=0
      ENDIF
   25 CONTINUE
      CALL RDPSRT(ITRN,HT,INDEX,.FALSE.)
      IF(DEBUG)WRITE(JOSTND,*)' INDEX = ',(INDEX(I),I=1,ITRN)
C
      SUMPIN = 0.
      HTMAX = 0.
      DO 30 I=1,ITRN
      ISRTI = INDEX(I)
      P = PROB(ISRTI)
      IF(DEBUG)WRITE(JOSTND,*)' IN FISHER CCPCT1, SUMPIN,ISRTI,P,HT,HTMA
     &X,TPROB= ',SUMPIN,ISRTI,P,HT(ISRTI),HTMAX,TPROB
      IF(DBH(ISRTI) .LT. 1.) GOTO 30
      IF(ICR(ISRTI) .LT. 31) GOTO 30
      IF(HT(ISRTI) .GE. HTMAX)THEN
        CCPCT=CCPCT + P*CRWDTH(ISRTI)**2.0
        SUMPIN = SUMPIN + P
        IF(DEBUG)WRITE(JOSTND,*)' ISRTI,P,CRWDTH,CCPCT,SUMPIN= ',
     &  ISRTI,P,CRWDTH(ISRTI),CCPCT,SUMPIN
      ENDIF
      IF(SUMPIN.GT.TPROB*0.10 .AND. HTMAX.EQ.0.)HTMAX = HT(ISRTI)*.50
   30 CONTINUE
      CCPCT = 100.0*CCPCT*0.785398/43560.
C----------
C  LOOP THROUGH TREES AND CALCULATE:
C  1) BASAL AREA IN SMALL TREES, 5-51 CENTIMETERS DBH
C     (BASM: SQUARE METERS/HA)
C  2) PERCENT CROWN COVER OF DOMINANT AND CODOMINANT TREES
C     (CCPCT: PERCENT, ALLOW FOR OVERLAP)
C  3) ARITHMETIC AVERAGE DIAMETER OF ALL HARDWOODS
C     (ADHW: CENTIMETERS)
C  4) DIAMETER OF THE LARGEST LIVE TREE IN THE STAND
C     (DMAX: CENTIMETERS)
C  5) DIAMETER OF THE LARGEST CONIFER SNAG IN THE STAND
C     (DSNMAX: CENTIMETERS)
C----------
```

```
      DO 90 I=1,ITRN
      ISPC = ISP(I)
      D = DBH(I)
      P = PROB(I)
      IF(D .GT. DMAX)DMAX=D
C
C     NOTE: IN THE DIAMETER SCREEN BELOW, WE ARE USING 5" AS THE LOWER
C           LIMIT INSTEAD OF 5 CM (1.9685") TO BE CONSISTENT WITH THE
C           WAY ANDREW GRAY (PNW-FIA) SAYS IT NEEDS TO BE CALCULATED
C           WHICH IS CONTRARY TO THE PUBLICATION. THIS MAY NEED TO BE
C           CHANGED.
C     IF(D.GE.1.9685 .AND. D.LT.20.0787)THEN
C
      IF(D.GE.5.0 .AND. D.LT.20.0787)THEN
        BASM = BASM + 0.0054542*P*D*D
      ENDIF
      IF(VVER(:2).EQ.'WS' .AND. (ISPC.EQ.7 .OR. ISPC.EQ.11))THEN
        ADHW=ADHW + D*P
        SUMTPA=SUMTPA + P
      ELSEIF(VVER(:2).EQ.'NC' .AND. (ISPC.EQ.5 .OR. ISPC.EQ.7 .OR.
     &       ISPC.EQ.8 .OR. ISPC.EQ.11))THEN
        ADHW=ADHW + D*P
        SUMTPA=SUMTPA + P
      ELSEIF(VVER(:2).EQ.'CA' .AND. ISPC.GE.26)THEN
        ADHW=ADHW + D*P
        SUMTPA=SUMTPA + P
      ELSEIF(VVER(:2).EQ.'SO' .AND. ((ISPC.GE.21 .AND. ISPC.LE.31) .OR.
     &       ISPC.EQ.33))THEN
        ADHW=ADHW + D*P
        SUMTPA=SUMTPA + P
      ENDIF
   90 CONTINUE
      IF(DEBUG)WRITE(JOSTND,*)' IN FISHER DMAX,ADHS,SUMTPA,BASM,CCPCT= '
     &,DMAX,ADHW,SUMTPA,BASM,CCPCT
C----------
C   CALCULATE:
C   5) DIAMETER OF THE LARGEST CONIFER SNAG IN THE STAND
C      (DSNMAX: CENTIMETERS)
C----------
      CALL FMEVMSN(DSNMAX)
      IF(DEBUG)WRITE(JOSTND,*)' IN FISHER DSNMAX= ',DSNMAX
C----------
C   CONVERT ENGLISH UNITS TO METRIC UNITS WHERE APPROPRIATE
C   PERCENT CROWN COVER SHOULD BE EQUIVALENT CALCULATED EITHER WAY
C   CALCULATE THE FISHER HABITAT SUITABILITY INDEX
C----------
      DMAX = DMAX*2.54
      DSNMAX = DSNMAX*2.54
```

```
      IF(SUMTPA .GT. 0.)THEN
        ADHW = (ADHW/SUMTPA)*2.54
      ELSE
        ADHW = 0.
      ENDIF
      BASM = BASM*0.2295643
      IF(DEBUG)WRITE(JOSTND,*)' IN FISHER, CCPCT,BASM,ADHW,DMAX,SLOPE,',
     &'DSNMAX= ',CCPCT,BASM,ADHW,DMAX,SLOPE,DSNMAX
C
      IF(CCPCT .GT. 0.)THEN
        X1=ALOG10(CCPCT)
      ELSE
        X1 = 0.
      ENDIF
      IF(BASM .GT. 0.)THEN
        X2=ALOG10(BASM)
      ELSE
        X2 = 0.
      ENDIF
      IF(ADHW .GT. 0.)THEN
        X3=ALOG10(ADHW)
      ELSE
        X3 = 0.
      ENDIF
      IF(DMAX .GT. 0.)THEN
        X4=ALOG10(DMAX)
      ELSE
        X4 = 0.
      ENDIF
      IF(SLOPE .GT. 0.)THEN
        X5=ALOG10(SLOPE*100.)
      ELSE
        X5 = 0.
      ENDIF
C
      TEMP = -22.1217941 + 2.461062*X1 + 2.15615937*X2 + 0.47133361*X3
     & + 4.55271635*X4 + 2.16130549*X5 + 0.00793579*DSNMAX
      FINDX=EXP(TEMP)/(1+EXP(TEMP))
C
  500 CONTINUE
      IF(DEBUG)WRITE(JOSTND,*)' LEAVING FISHER, TEMP,FINDX= ',TEMP,FINDX
      RETURN
```

This publication is available online at http://www.fs.fed.us/psw/. You may also order additional copies of it by sending your mailing information in label form through one of the following means. Please specify the publication title and series number.

Fort Collins Service Center

Web site	http://www.fs.fed.us/psw/
Telephone	(970) 498-1392
FAX	(970) 498-1122
E-mail	rschneider@fs.fed.us
Mailing address	Publications Distribution
	Rocky Mountain Research Station
	240 West Prospect Road
	Fort Collins, CO 80526-2098

Pacific Southwest Research Station
800 Buchanan Street
Albany, CA 94710

U.S. Department of Agriculture
Pacific Northwest Research Station
333 SW First Avenue
P.O. Box 3890
Portland, OR 97208-3890

Official Business
Penalty for Private Use, $300

www.ingramcontent.com/pod-product-compliance
Lightning Source LLC
Chambersburg PA
CBHW082201290526
45794CB00008B/3384

*9 7 8 1 4 8 0 1 6 3 6 0 7 *